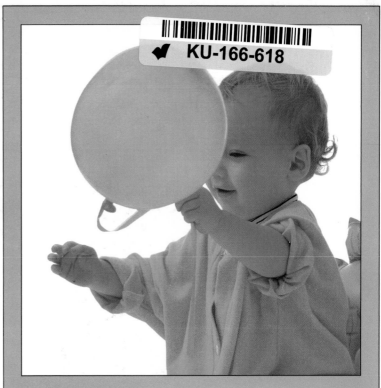

For darling Alan, and my two
lovely children, Harriet and Tom

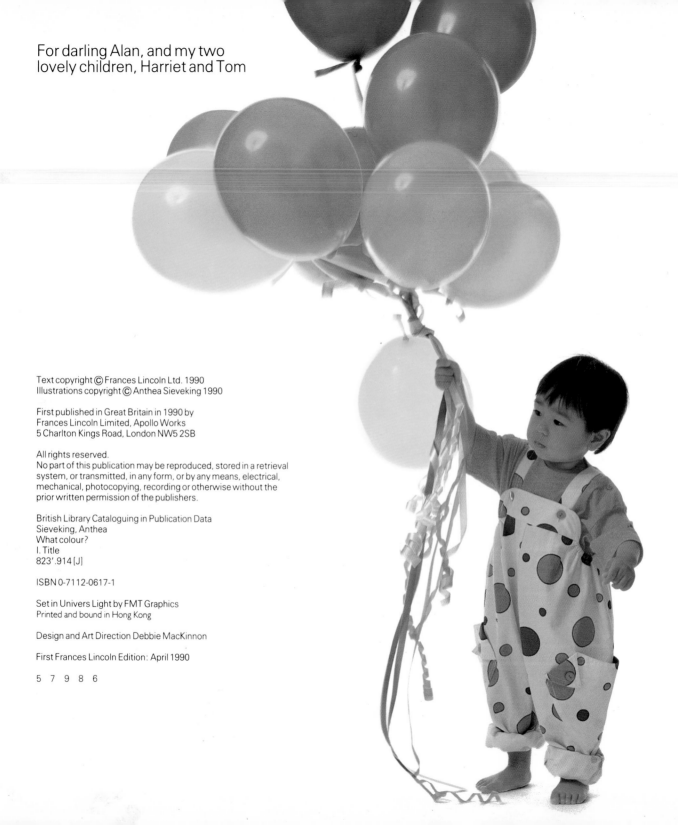

First published in Great Britain in 1990 by
Frances Lincoln Limited, Apollo Works
5 Charlton Kings Road, London NW5 2SB

British Library Cataloguing in Publication Data
Sieveking, Anthea
What colour?
I. Title
823'.914 [J]

ISBN 0-7112-0617-1

Set in Univers Light by FMT Graphics
Printed and bound in Hong Kong

Design and Art Direction Debbie MacKinnon

First Frances Lincoln Edition: April 1990

5 7 9 8 6

WHAT COLOUR?

Photographs by Anthea Sieveking

FRANCES LINCOLN

What colour is Chiau Pheng's raincoat?

Red

raincoat

rainhat

umbrella

boots

What colour is Louis' balloon?

Orange

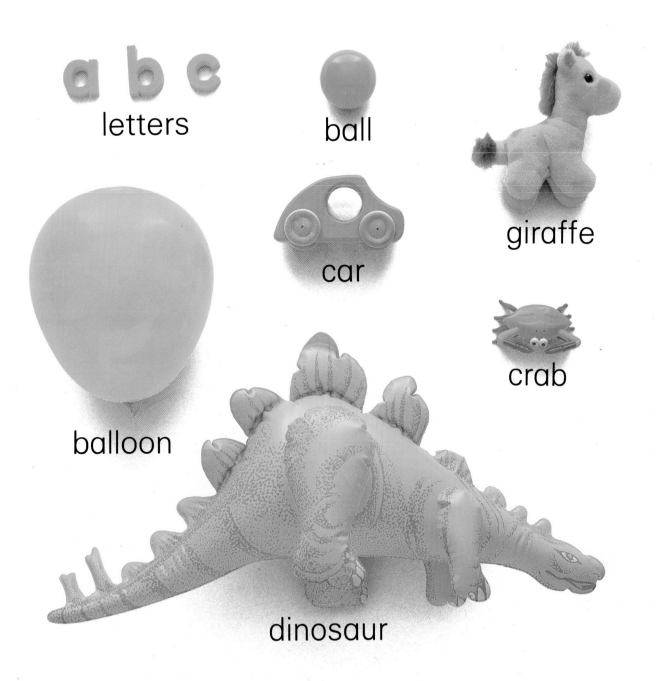

letters

ball

giraffe

car

crab

balloon

dinosaur

What colour is Sabrina's shampoo?

Yellow

toothbrush

boat

shampoo

duck

sponge

soap

flannel

What colour is Daniel's apple?

Green

apple

peas

green pepper

beans

courgette

lettuce

What colour is Grace's cup?

Blue

spoon

fork

cup

bunny

plate

What colour is Jessica's pig?

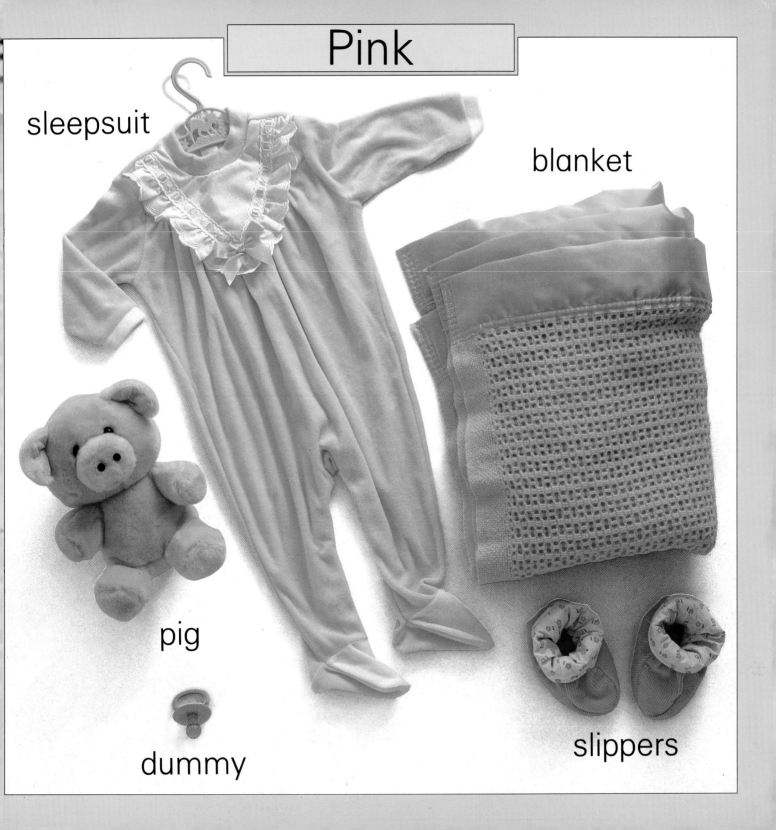

Pink

sleepsuit

blanket

pig

dummy

slippers

What colour are Sophie's and Zoe's hats?

Black

cat

gloves

necklace

hat

Daddy's shoes

What colour is Lorelle's teddy?

White

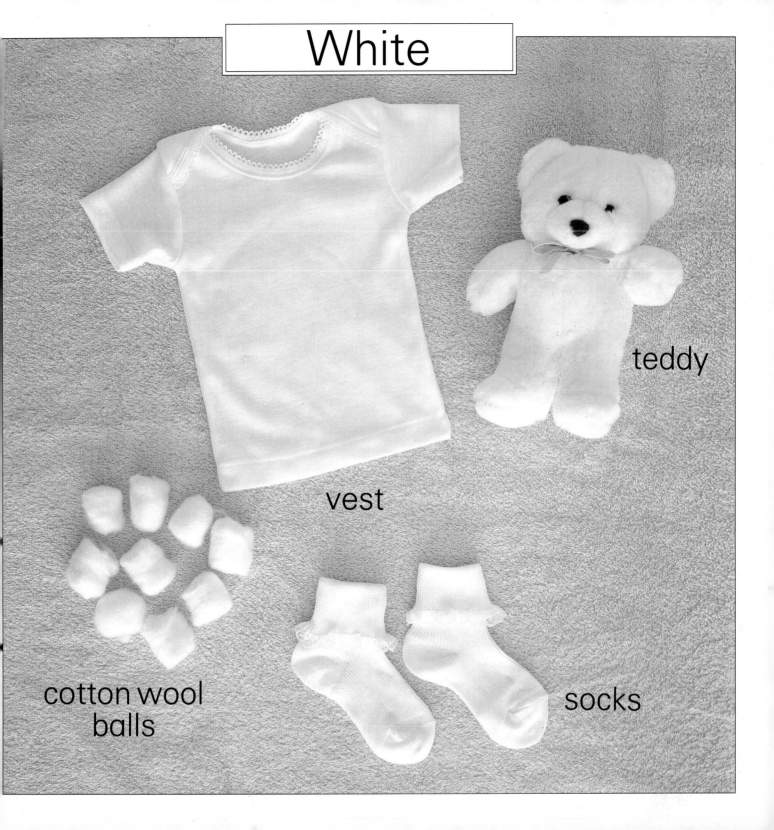

teddy

vest

cotton wool
balls

socks